I3
signed

The Armpit of Desire

The Armpit of Desire

Poems by
Scott Siders

iUniverse, Inc.
New York Lincoln Shanghai

The Armpit of Desire

iUniverse books may be ordered through booksellers or by contacting:

iUniverse
2021 Pine Lake Road, Suite 100
Lincoln, NE 68512
www.iuniverse.com
1-800-Authors (1-800-288-4677)

Cover painting: *Desire* by Stephanie von Reckers, 2005, oil on canvas
Cover design by Stephanie von Reckers
Author photograph by Allison Riley

ISBN-13: 978-0-595-36882-2 (pbk)
ISBN-13: 978-0-595-81295-0 (ebk)
ISBN-10: 0-595-36882-4 (pbk)
ISBN-10: 0-595-81295-3 (ebk)

Printed in the United States of America

for Allison

The words barely begin
to match the desire.

> ~from "A Long Conversation"
> by Adrienne Rich

Until we say the truth, there can be no tenderness.
As long as there is desire, we will not be safe.

> ~from "Adam and Eve"
> by Tony Hoagland

All the things I can talk about
mean nothing to me.

> ~from "Vice"
> by Amiri Baraka

Contents

Acknowledgements

With thanks to the editors of the following journals in which these poems (some in earlier versions) first appeared:

Into the Teeth of the Wind (Volume I, Issue 3): "Somewhere More Familiar"
The Mississippi Review (Volume 32): "The Right Light"
Strategic Confusion (Volume I, Issue II): "We Do Not Make Love"
Strategic Confusion (Volume II, Issue I): "Offering"

"Last New Look" and "Seven Days in October" first appeared on the Ten Stories Tall CD *Next of Kin*.

ARMED WITH WHAT WE KNOW

THE RIGHT LIGHT

*...We wear the river's light on our hands, that other
river, all border, outside, beyond. Just look at that man
waving to his wife, the gluey light webbed about fingers*

*leaking towards hers, hers towards his,—a shivering frequency
that holds, wants to go on, the giving light of our hands,
haloing the object, the object that endures...*

~from "Light"
by Mark Irwin

1. A Gift You Can Use

In the subtle light of afternoon, you find
a package at your doorstep. Inside the box
someone has drawn a rough sketch of you.
Though the room has lost
its light, at a glance it's obvious
how much time & work went into the drawing
& redrawing of your head.
Between smudges, your mouth
has formed a river. It opens your face.

2. Random Scenes from a Mistaken Adulthood

Scene 1: September

Somewhere on a dark street
a man with a pocket of wadded-up cash
walks with dry hands pressing

presidents as if in no hurry at all, as if
liquor stores stay open all
night, as if bar-women are bar-women

in the morning, as if the right
light makes all the difference, as if nothing
gives way if you don't give in.

Scene 2: October

If it wasn't for the endless
pelting of rain, unsigned
letters. If it wasn't for
the tremble of her voice,
the sound of wind brushing
leaves against her house.
If it wasn't for the slow
burn of night, this empty block
& flickering streetlight.
If it wasn't for the hours
spent pinned to the radio,
her shadow in the upstairs
bedroom window—I'd fire up
this Chevy & drive unswerving
out of here, leaving this town
without a goodbye, without
a first or last kiss…

Scene 3: November

Sun on snow. Rivers build.
Small animals blink & burrow.

A man on a street borrows
change for a meter. A woman

takes change from a black
purse. This side of town is

threatening to break. Dinner
is only as good as lunch.

Out on the parkway the drive
is unraveling. There goes a river.

3. A Letter to My Parents on the Subject of Death

In another life we might know
why we shrivel, forget. A weight
lifts. A woman sweats out a son.
A chair, untouched for years, breaks

in the rocking. A man must work with wood.
Chop. Chop. There is never enough. Would
it be better to dodge our roles? No.
Why do we live like this? Wait.
A man loads a truck in the sun.
Drive. Drive. Light eases up, brakes.

P.S. If I'm taken before you, promise
     to eat cake at my wake.

4. Skinvention

Scene 1: First Wounding

Outside a cafe a man waves
his hands in the face of another man. His hair
rounds the side of his head: a halo
of hair. He wipes sweat from his scalp.
The other man can't stop looking
disinterested. Money must not be involved.

A woman's name is shouted.
From across the street you can see
she's no lady: see the red hooker-boots
zipped up to the knee? See the make-up
covering the make-up? A car cuts to the curb.
A man waves & waves & waves his hands.

Scene 2: The Body as Braille

Sometime in the future a dark room.
Two bodies escape from sleep.
A hand finds a face.
An index finger slides across a chest, over a stomach.
The slow fingering of dust along the curve of a sportscar.
The surplus of eyes.
A single white curtain gyrating on a window.
A tongue forgetting.
An unraveling of legs.
Sweat of the mind.
A body pressed to another in movement.
A border built by gravity.
Two books read. One book written.

After Before

        Because its sound licks the soft interior
of your body, but you can't
        touch it. Because, when you could fit

in the palm of your father's hand, a neighbor
        saw you for the first time
and told his wife he didn't know babies could be

        ugly. Because your mother used to whisper
in your tiny ears, and oh, if
        only you could find the space those words

fell in, you'd repeat them like a mantra until
        they wore a hole in your
throat. Because of the way you can't shake

        your bad reputation. Because you miss
understanding. Because
        there's a place where all spare change

goes. Because you never climbed trees when
        you were small, or even
thought of it. Because there is a hole beneath

        the belly of a tree downtown, a hole
full of holes, bending
        into a root system that leads to the thick

underside of an old stretch of asphalt somewhere
        where you now live.
Because the city has a throat and is humming.

        Because even machines in the most
desperate state of disrepair
        click into a rhythm you can get used to.

Seven Days in October

1.

What they told us is not true.
There is no right way to speak
and there is beauty in the way you sign
your name. This is no time for switching
lights on. A scar is a tattoo. My body
is ornamental. Hands are for writing on.
There is nothing I can say to you.

2.

The mirror in the kitchen finally
shattered into little glass lights.
Morning shadows the wall
the way the space between us
grows into itself, the way
it's the kind of day you can look up
and see even the sun has an edge.

3.

The stamp on the back of your hand
reminds me of jawbreakers
and summer sweat in the grass, a time
somewhere west of here
when it was okay to kiss anyone
for any reason, alright to wave
like the world was coming to an end.

4.

A tongue is all it takes. A finger
loose on a bald head, a fallen
eyelash, a nose always on the clock.
There is nothing they can do to us
we haven't already done
to ourselves, and for this reason
the work will go on without us.

5.

It's not raindrops fattening
on a windowpane.
It's the way paint on the street
weathers, the way, at night, steam
rises from the street, the way
a street is the roof of a house
that always needs fixing.

6.

We were born dying.
This is no time for a weather report.
October is early this year, the moon
beginning to rust
and clouds billowing as if heaven's on fire.
Reality is still in the details.
One can find religion in brooding.

7.

Our breath eases into smoke
and everywhere the sound of words
shivering, embarrassed
even as they leave our mouths.
The little lives we know
are all we have, and we have them until
they will have nothing more to do with us.

Moving In

To begin, you paint the windows
black. You use the straight
side of the right hand, firmly
working paint in small, obtuse
swervings of the wrist, the tips
of your fingers evening
thick globules into one corner

and then another. You carry
a flashlight through the widening
dark of the house, wiping paint
across your torso in one long
swipe. You climb a ladder
to the third floor's high window.
Spider-wary, you spray

light on the ceiling, clutching
the fifth rung from the top.
An abandoned web leans
in on itself. You paw at it, tearing
thread from sinuous thread.
Quick, like the very essence
of the body of fear, you rub

the window black. Outside
hours are occurring. Candles
are lit: little stars burning about you.
You shed your clothing, the body's
ornaments, and burn every shred
of the body's memory. The door
is banged on—more like

attacked. Whoever it is
must have followed you, if only
to see how you made out.
Finally all is silent. You lie
spread-eagled on the living room's
wooden floor, your face
no longer your own. Wrists

and ankles are heavy and chained
to an invisible rack, pressure
steadily increasing, pulled by every
gasping dark corner of the room.
Hear the crank click again
and again, every notch a testimony?
Smell the contraption's rusty

neglect? Feel the desire of paint
gripping windows, blood straining
from the ends of the body?
Now your eyes are little lights.
If you hold your mouth just right
your tongue becomes electric.
Feel the body's trembling?

You've done this to yourself.

WE DO NOT MAKE LOVE

Instead, I balance a ceramic red bowl
upside down on the curve
of your thigh. Your slight, callused hands
have shaped and painted it.
My legs wrap your waist. Our hair grows
together. We are old. I hold
the bowl up openside above your ears.
I have filled it with you. I eat
and eat. You loosen your eyes. There is
no climate. It is good. My face
dips like an animal to water. The room
pounds in gasping sounds
of my tongue smacking. The bowl empties.
We've waited years for this.

WISHING

1. The Wishing Bone

Sprung from the head of a river
or swept up by the current. What
might move, if only to escape
the nothing that isn't there?
The way this spot of torn skin
fits in the light. How, when you
walk towards me, it feels like

you're walking away. Stuck in this—
the being bone always wishing,
tallying sleep in the waking hours.
The way feathers touch each other
in a pillow. Every bone in your body
creaks in unison, a choir of bones
in a house of air. The way a scar

is always a scar. To strip a chicken
of its skin, its wishbone a bone
to be coveted, the treasure that lies
within. What secret, what desire
minds the missing? What guts.
Knuckle to knuckle. Eyes on eyes.
The way it bends before it breaks.

2. The Wishing Hour

It has its way of sneaking up on you in the sleep of your dreams.
Every second of every minute is spent digesting, preparing.
The heat or frigidity of night is its happening, its shine.
Somewhere in the world it's doing its work right now.
It has no use for clocks, no use for the prodding human hand.
Each moment devolves into what it takes, what it gives.
Every night the short possession, the resolve of what moves us.
Hollow but heavy, the way a wall connects, adapts.
The grinding of dreams, the way to grease a machine.

A watershed, a body of soil evolving into mud, where it goes.
The slow burn of ash is the secret, if only alive in the belly's pit.
Whenever you wake, sweating in your bed, you've interrupted it.

3. The Wishing Well

A stone well dug deep in the earth, a boy-child still brimming with hope, shirt-less in a grassy field, tipping his chest over the rough edge of stone, his wide-eyed stare into the watery dark of the well, holding a quarter, an entire allowance, the silence of wishing, the secret, a time to be barefoot, feathery clouds moving furiously west, fast enough to draw eyes, the first moments of a sprint. When dusk hits the sky sheds.

4. The Wishers

In the meantime we're learning
to lie. Born upside-down
and left-handed. Hand over
handshake. Alone in this
and people everywhere. Watch
where you step. The endless
search for a space to lie

your head. In a garden
an old woman in a blue dress
wears gloves made for work.
She kneels on bony knees and plucks
spiny roots from the earth.
Vigilance, she says, is the way
to God. The path to heaven

is pocked with weeds.
This part of the country has seen
its share of digging. Tumbleweeds
spin their way free of the fences.
Each day is a flash of light
hitched to the gravity
of this place, this island of sky
where even geese fly alone.

EVERYTHING TOMATO

At the brink of almost, I position myself
                    for a breakthrough in style.
            Start by blowing through beer bottles.
I use you to get to the get to. I live between
                    heavy machinery and medieval

monkeys. Tease. To hell with sentimentality:
                    move to the country and buy
            a farm. Possibility of disaster: everything
tomato. As usual, I have no excuse. Here's one:
                    I saw my mother vomit once

and that was enough for me. We've all become
                    women and that's that. No men
            left to speak of. We're all philosophical
and no nonsense. They don't need us anymore.
                    Insemination is everywhere

and artificial. A red bowl of fruit on a plastic
                    table: go ahead and eat. Hang
            like patterned drapes in some mother's
living room. Believe. I have scissors. Let's cut.
                    I'm in charge, here. You're

synthesized. Draw your name on my body in big
                    fat letters. Not just there.
            There. Here: take this spoon and dig.
If the eye is a window, you must be embarrassed
                    as hell. It doesn't work that way:

first the eyeball, then the spoon. We learn
                    like we lie and we like to learn.
            Yesterday I walked down a gravel road.
Cars raced by and dust fingered itself on my face.
                    Every other car was a father

and not one stopped. My thumb broke. I was ten
                    stories tall. I walked a straight line
            out into another country and into a garden,

the soles of my shoes worn through and baby
              copper blisters being born. Through

the dust my eyes stretched into the wild symmetry
              of the field. Bared to the moist soil,
        seeping into the earth little by little, my toes
softened the blow for the blisters. The garden grew
           red on red: everything tomato.

Spout

Rain has ripped the house for weeks. Our roof was built for a thing much smaller than its body, its bared rooms. The spout bone sinks into its stone socket foundation. The house shakes. When it began, rain slid from crumbling slopes, smacking the yard. Sometime in early morning, in the ache of black streets, rain began its slow dive into shallow rooms. We were smart with our buckets and pots. Soon

the yard gives way. Buckets and pots overflow and we howl at the sight of it. Rain screams down walls. The water level rises and our furniture with it. We lie in bed, our wooden raft, navigating the house. Everywhere the constant plodding of water echoing water. A swelling den and empty study: somewhere below

a heap of letters. Above us a dark ceiling hangs. It's impossible to see. We grow cold. Day never comes. Our bodies slop together. We bang through rooms. Rain hammers on, an alarm. There is no sound until we break it, choking on hollow bellies. Water threatens tops of windows. Idea of death: noise. And so it is, and so it shall be. I tear into you. One of us must beat this.

SOMEWHERE MORE FAMILIAR

*There are so many domains. And [she] doesn't know it
yet, but she's traveling through time at a ferocious rate. She's
going to live in another world. She's going to be someone's flower.*

~from "Domains"
by Albert Goldbarth

for Annabel

I found her on the sharp edge of this town.
This girl, she has eyes like manhole covers.
She says I make her feel younger than she is
when we lie together on the bed her father made
with the skill of his arrogant hands. This girl,
she's a sidewalk. She sees men in the weight
of jackhammers. They've cracked her surface
and flooded in like promises. She aged
on a street where secrets made puddles, and she
drenched herself in them. This girl, she's what's
left after the rain. Years ago, her father
loved her in strange places. She hears he still
breathes in this city. He's a sonofanother
father who loved like that, who gave his children
pizza, money for the movies, and penis
twice a week while the neighborhood slept.

This girl, she remembers that man
like a ten-car-pile-up. When I slide my fingers
through her hair, she disappears in those puddles.
She sees the claws. She just sees the claws.
When the moon holds her eyes the way
the very old hold photographs, she wraps herself
around me with the determination of a child.
Sometimes, in the hours before morning, I find
myself on top of her, holding her chin against mine.
She wakes in a tremble, her arms tense
with the exhaustion of dreams. She feels the weight,
the smell of a man and the press of a mattress.

the weight the
            weight the weight
                        the weight

This girl, her body was sworn to puddles.
Mud spread its fingers and held her close, pulled
her in until her life came down to a splash
on that bed. He must have believed in her.
She was a project, his life's work. He controlled
the doorknobs of that house. He owned everything
inside. His footsteps in the hall were a warning.
She would prepare herself. The door would swing
open and he'd appear like he belonged, poker-faced
and battle-ready. He'd work in silence. She'd dig
her fingers in the sheet, fix her eyes on the imprint
of the moon stretched along the folds of the curtain.

The weight of the morning took her somewhere
more familiar. She'd wash out her eyes in the rush
of the shower, the water he paid for. I can see her
at the breakfast table, the omelets her mother made,
her brother learning to make knots of shoelaces.
And next to her, with the newspaper sprawled across
the table, that man would ask her how she slept.
Her tangled yellow hair would be brushed straight
by then. She'd tell him *Good, daddy. Good.*
Then her eyes would find the clock, the minutes
she'd wait for the school bus.
                        At night, when shadows
own the room, she curls up like old shoes who've
known the depth of puddles. I tell her it's as if she'd
fled a foreign war and returned somewhere more
familiar, escaped the stench of that place, the quick
breaths of those early mornings. Wars are fought
in the minds of the ones who know winning
isn't an option, who know survival is the only weapon.
Rain from that war dried up years ago, but his heavy
voice still holds her like a whispering lover. This girl,
she says it was always like this. She closes her eyes
and fades away to somewhere more familiar, not
remembering the hush of daddy, the eyes of daddy,
the weight of daddy, the dried wounds on her thighs—
the wild snoring of mother in the next room.

APRIL

1.
is a boxcar, wood-burnt black, brown
steel held together still by a welder's
handshake. It's true that my grandfather

died here, one mile north and two miles
east from where his mother, too old

2.
to give birth, gave her life in
giving his. They say he didn't cry until
the third day. His father had seen

the bottom of one too many bottles.
He missed out on the coming and going

3.
of lives. He was never found.
My grandfather never looked for him.
The country roads in that sweaty

state, those roads cutting through
cornfields, running on dust upon dust

4.
forever in all directions, wherever
or however a man makes it from one
end of his life to the other, to catch

a train, to steal a car, if only
to walk, is something worth doing

5.
if growing old is something worth
getting to. Before he died
my grandfather spoke of his mother

as if he knew her, as if she was the woman
in the blue dress, sweating, hunched

6.

over a stove, humming quietly
to herself, setting the table, pouring
the milk, the one next to his bed

at night, her calloused hand waving
through his hair, saying goodnight.

7.

April is a green husk of corn, brown
and withered at its ends, one on top
of another in a white, five-gallon

bucket. It's true that my grandmother
was the oldest and bravest of seven

8.

sisters. She once put her body
between her father and her youngest
sister. He had a way with words

when he was clutching a bottle.
He almost always had a way

9.

with words. Bruises for everyone.
He wanted a boy-child.
"Seven goddamn girls," he would

say, "and not one boy. This family
is cursed." He worked very

10.

hard, in spite of his misfortune.
My grandmother left school for good
after the eighth grade. The home

needed her. She traded algebra
for baking bread, English for washing

11.

dishes, earth science for tomato-
picking, corn-shucking, potato-
peeling. My grandmother helped

ease her mother's heat-tremors.
She helped cook her father's

12.

meat and potatoes. When the others
were old enough, the light of the first
of seven sisters tried to leave that house

as if any one star can ever escape
Cassiopeia, as if her father could.

13.

April is a muscle-car drag-racing
another muscle-car down a newly
paved road, when muscle-cars

were ordinary cars. It's true
that my father has owned

14.

exactly the same number of cars
as years he has lived. If you ask him
he'll tell you he was a natural-born

hell-raiser. In those days, in that
town, if the cops caught you

15.

drinking and drag-racing, they'd pour out
your beer and tell you to go
home. Those cars held themselves

together on the same steel that still
holds that boxcar together, the same

16.

steel my father sells to this day.
To run from your past is to deny
yourself a future constructed

from anything worth being
welded together, or so my father

17.

said once, in not so many words.
Out on the open road, adrift
on a motorcycle, before I could drive

or even think of it, I would hold
my body against his, leaning

18.

into the turns instinctually, as if
what he'd done so many years
back, set me on my way, as if

anything I do repeats, but not
by design, not because I had to.

19.

April is a long walk alone
through a city of empty streets
in the middle of night when only

space-light shines the way. It's true
that my mother has suffered. Her mind

20.

is and is not the explanation
of why the where the what
and how we ended up

like this. There is a cul-de-sac
in a neighborhood where we

21.

lived once, and a baby-sitter there
who did unmentionable things.
My mother has done nothing

but work for me her entire
life. She will die a younger woman

22.

because of me. Is that the sacrifice
a mother must make? Do mothers
become martyrs when they die?

She used to tend her garden like
my grandmother, her hands back

23.

and forth between what would live
and what wouldn't, weeds ripped
away like so many scabs. Gardens move on

with generations, from a hungry face
smudged with mud to a face sunburned

24.

red, glowing in the surprise of flowers.
Still, mothers bear the heat of it all, marching
steadily on, as if sweat was made only

for them, as if we all grow up to prove
our worth, our purpose for their pain.

25.

April is not the cruelest month.
Spring is a thing for dead poets.
It's true that I've spent an entire day

on my grandfather's grave.
I find myself in this part of the country

26.
so rarely, and a cemetery seemed
to be a natural place to be in spring.
Armed with what we know

we shuffle our way out, shooing
whatever breath's left into cars

27.
and out of towns. When my grandfather
died, we set him in the ground
right here. That old boxcar on the other

side of the cemetery fence is enough
to remind me of traveling, enough

28.
to be here, writing this history
down, my ancestors over my shoulder
and whispering. I cross my heart

and say no prayer.
My grandfather's old bones frame

29.
the space where we planted him.
Out here, along this old dirt
road, I feel the hunger in my gut

and look out beyond the fence
at a garden some mother

30.
is tending. It's barely possible to read
what's been chiseled into stone.
I get this notion I should learn to weld

steel, or at least use my hands more.
My breath is in the weeds and moving on.

THE DISEMBODIED
GROAN

OFFERING

out of pockets brimming with sweat & the offering \ got
        loose in my pants \ tangled grit & ornaments \ *i got*
        buckets of paint & no brush \ unconditioned on nerved
        bones \ insulation advised with warning \ blur
        is ordinary & expected \ move it along \ myopia
        of schizophallic tendencies \ gradual buzz \ indigestion
        of the body classes \ lull out the somehow in spastic
        glimmers \ *this girl i know she wears her tits outside*
        her bra she's post-feminist
out of percolated page \ from organ to organism \ after
        vision of ape on iceberg \ before revision of boy on
        blueprint \ in daylight an ordinary bird \ ornithological-
        bound or binding \ near a pond after rain \ a place
        i go to sometimes \ some cuts are unrecognizable \ some
        birds can't fly! \ some people can't speak \ out of
        a hollow log a hound dog \ eyes like little lights
        approaching dark \ tails say more than saying \ tail plus
        wag equals personality (emotional mindstate) \ dogs
        have emotional mindstates! \ it's dogality \ simple &
        refined \ no pretense \ some dogs can run really
        fast! \ *if i had a choice i'd choose a tail over wings any*
        day \ *anyone can get on an airplane* \ doggish \ even
        nebraska is beautiful from the air
out of gut again \ we reach in our pockets & pull out
        touché \ all night we move throbbing asses over
        cracked blacktop \ crickets like downbeat hiccups
        singing us through turnstyles of desire \ *it's fifty for*
        a bj \ *twenty for a handjob* \ *one hundred for straight*
        sex \ smiling & fingering of wallet \ *i'm in for*
        fifty \ there's a premium on last impressions \ every
        where postmodern american hookers \ necessary
        like travel is necessary \ he want it here \ him move
        between fenders \ him unzip \ she suck suck suck \ he
        make her remember he got big one \ him swagger on
        street with cock slung over shoulder
out of matisse \ from signified to drool \ it was certain from
        the beginning \ she would have no face \ what

without a face can the body mean? \ can a right leg rub
over a left & mean more? \ are we meant to notice
its stomach in various guises? \ always breasts breasts
breasts \ in order to be able to go on a man must find
a set of eyes \ hands in ceiling walls \ but before there
were sperm there was necklace & thick body dripping
down body \ a fish is enough to paint \ landscapes may
overwhelm \ underneath in the dark colors begin \ a girl
is a pattern & a room no escape
out of spoonfeeding into rinsewater \ desire determines
_____ \ *it rains all week* \ *fall is so beautiful*
because everything dies & i can relate to that \ half-in
half-out of water they repeat exacerbate \ the word
exacerbate like we are \ *hardboiled* \ he agrees
though it isn't what he means for it to mean so \ to hell
with it maybe but hell is on the move \ it isn't yours
anymore \ we're all in the gutter but some of us are
laughing \ desire is red (read) again \ on the
verge \ *the only way to get rid of a temptation is to*
yield to it so says oscar wilde \ out of color \ from
the mouth of dislocation \ into the meat of the
meeting of us \ not u.s. \ this sway of states like the
bend/break of twigs in late october \ us is we when in
little death \ this not little \ so says man off boat
from xanadu \ he got mean cock & madness on
mind \ traveling again
out of a test of how my hand works now \ unwrenched
& in an ear \ hear me cuss from dipstick to
tiger-fucker \ in between seams \ there is tragedy
in all this understanding \ here is the journal of
imaginary fragments \ shoestring \ cell \ lone pine in
wilderness \ oh how romantic the wilderness! \ *it's all*
calculated negation \ *wind is to cloud as water is*
to dirt \ mathematics isn't for the squeamish \ this is
not a time for flinching \ out of the trunk & into the
closet \ reflex of shrill \ however wirebound however
muscular
out of supply \ must make others understand i don't
need them \ i've been here all their lives \ a stream i
go to sometimes \ him grab wild by balls him

bareass splash \ noise like noise arrives \ scribble
scribble scribble \ if there is extra \ him swim with
fishes him grow gills \ in a room an examination &
no desks \ him get good grade him go far \ portrait
of dough-people with tentacles \ sideplate of
testicles \ him not right him round \ bass floating
out of a pond \ amputate like this \ regurgitation of
blown glass \ new developments of the lost
words \ scleroma \ grosbeak \ unsling \ toxicity
is right \ plummet from sky a sustaining \ empire of
no \ sharpen \ which way vacancy \ however
reconsider \ window inspectors everywhere &
buffalo \ here come the fishboats \ there go captain
category \ him wet on rock still proclaiming
out of numbered woodgrain \ take then these
testicles \ i've dulled all the knives \ driving way
out west \ red on dry \ all hotels built for the
offering \ more towels please & room service \ here
take this if you need it please pass it along \ him
get rich on slots him hand nice fit \ driving
again \ this way no stop or firelight \ them flashers
coming \ she's a sweater i want here always \ erase
or rarely with scissors \ fingernails like sweaty
meat \ gnaw gnaw gnaw \ i'm eating myself again
out of a sleeping binge \ half-life of dreams \ boxes
piled up in little laboratories & experiments \ exhibit
A the six inch makes dixie cup offering on
gut \ exhibit B the eight inch makes bowling bag
offering on headboard \ exhibit C the ten inch makes
dumptruck offering on broad side of barn \ there sits
oregano \ glass jars arranged on countertop \ *you
stimulate my bowels* \ all week the stench of reborn
chickens \ sever right wing then left \ quivering pure
body mixed in milk sweet honey \ we'll be going
to a live feed this segment \ boy on bike breaks
nuts \ aborigines at eleven \ satisfaction guaranteed
out of summer \ the virgin mary appears on the back of
roadsigns in mexico \ we spent six hundred
dollars & switched buses six times \ obviously her or
not acting \ i've been looking at you i've been

windows \ how strange him say she appeared to me
& let's just say she ain't a virgin anymore \ her
like it tender \ i'm blessed & there are
precedents \ *alas i am dying beyond my means*
so says oscar wilde \ out of the mouth & onto
the red \ i stole a paintbrush & chopped off my
hands

Last New Look

After(words)
I am lost
(found), a great

beast on the move (no,
you can't see it). It takes
passion (don't forget to use

protection). Think taxi
Think taxi Think taxi Think
know-how (know how

to think). The best
aphrodisiac is still
on the move. I am

a new animal (the child
grows out of everything).
We're all searching

for a map. There must be
a map. I wear
a picture of my shoe

on my shoe, keep
a picture of Dr. Ruth
in my wallet. I am

(she is) experience-
based. I live a groove
agenda (you gotta be

aggressive, your head's gotta
spin). It takes passion.
We are great

beasts (the child grows
out of everything).
I am found

(lost), dangling
in guts. I am coming
where your mother

was coming from. Eat in.
Don't drive. Don't go
anywhere. I've worried

enough. Information
is forgetfulness. Clear
control feels like going off-

road, looks like the greatest
risk going. No,
you can't see it. Think

taxi. You are following
the nomadic male
(the child grows out

of everything). I am
strung out in the margin
(of the margin). I am lost

again (outside the buffer
zone). We're down
to you. We are great

beasts (it takes
passion). I am crawling
through you (you crawl

through a silhouette
of yourself). I am
forcing my eyes open

with your hands. I am
on the move. This is
everything you missed.

Self Portrait With Straw Hat

I am a passionate creature, destined to do
a number of more or less stupid things
which later on I will have more or less to regret.

~Vincent Van Gogh

They come to me in sleek, black dresses, the very rich.
I don't remember their eyes this way, deep
blue like the curtains in this room. Their fingers, sharp
as new money, curl against their palms. I could almost
fear them. A crowd forms. Children stare. They lean
forward on toes, careful to keep a distance. Necks tense up
and eyes get big as houses. They must have needed this.
I want to reach out and touch them just to feel
the sensation. The lines in their faces are growing.
They've come here for some understanding, some final
shot at grace. That night has come down to this.
We met in the flash of light, the patter of feet.
It was supposed to be easy and quick. I learned the exits
and locks, the alarms. The old man must have heard me
pause too long to admire it. I swear it was like the movies.
I was so good. I was professional. He must have had
a feeling, one of those fierce moments when you wake up
and just know something's happened. Something bad.
I heard him remember his gun. In one movement
I had Van Gogh off the wall and into the shadows.
The old man was grunting and bursting through every door.
He must have thought he was quiet. I thought
I'd been careful. Then his footsteps neared that room.
It was the last of the house. I'd waited five minutes.
I had to be calm. Haste will kill you faster than doubt.
Finally he exploded into the room like a younger man.
The light hit me. I had no choice. I fired twice.
His flashlight bounced at his feet. His back
smacked the wall. He let me have it on the way
down. He was good with a gun. He was professional.
Then the cries of the wife and children, thunder on the stairs.
Van Gogh was alive next to me on the floor.
I held him close, like a woman, his eyes fixed on mine.

I never saw the old man's eyes, never held his skin
so close as the bullet that grabbed me in that room,
splattering the face of Van Gogh. The old man
said nothing, slumped against the wall, his pistol
in his lap. His light splashed my blurry silhouette on the wall.
Van Gogh and I glowed in the terrified eyes of that woman.
She held his head against her breast like I clung to Van Gogh—
like, today, her arms hold her children close to her body.
And now it looks as if one of them might touch me.

INFERRING

in the absolute uncertainty \ admit eight & negotiate
      seven \ perpetual obscurity of daylight \ the fine
      line of define \ terrestrial lightning & the whole
      world fingering god \ a drain built for the hell
      of it \ to practice a chin-up \ always a hiccup
      away from perfect \ a mushroom cloud pretty
      at dusk \ a chance to purchase dirt & your father
      dreaming \ to learn to spit properly \ everywhere
      the tools of discontent \ to skin a fish with hang-
      nails \ try try try \ an attempt to sneak by all
      odds \ a clever line of defense \ last man standing
      or dead man walking \ to be a snake or annoy
      a pet \ boys will be bombing \ find a word
      that rhymes with orange
in the mood to breathe \ red food coloring soaking up
      the small of your back \ what you have to do
      & no more \ an exhibition featuring animals
      as artists or otherwise undercover \ humming
      in the black box & blinking \ if they speak
      spanish in spain \ turtles back from the war
      & shell-shocked \ the outer space between cars
      in a strip mall parking lot \ assume people are
      funny until you meet them \ full to the brim with
      disappointments \ inquisition of the boom & babies
      rampant in this part of town \ they're making
      more of them every day \ a race not erase \ a way
      to carve stars on your chest & glow \ a witness
      acting \ a state of mind not real estate \ a motion
      to dismiss \ beg beg beg
in the scene & whispering a way out \ a country comfortable
      with demolition \ rain replacing emotion \ a way to
      tell time in the dark \ all night the bugs & dusty
      moon \ ready to ship to some woman \ anything buried
      a reason to grow \ the taste & texture of beans
      the same anywhere \ food always the subject \ accept
      or except the rich \ wait to access not excess
      weight \ way too much way too soon \ a hell of a lot

of people with big bones \ eat eat eat \ a steady diet
a study of stretch-marks \ lines on the body like
tributaries going nowhere fast \ tunneling out
& ahead of the curve \ a starving ecosystem \ waiting
for the screaming flush
in the deep water \ a great white shark allergic to fish & sad
 · about seaweed \ however unbelievable the rogue seed
burrows \ visibility is sworn off \ roadblocks & orange
at every turn \ a 400-pound gorilla & four horsemen
guerrilla fighting \ if not for the hollering \ an existence
essential not existential \ a way to read a book
wrong \ a holding of breath for the worst \ skin-
tight water like sky but wet \ born into this mess
& dreaming \ sleep sleep sleep \ an area in arizona
that doesn't feel like hell \ do what you're told
& put on a happy face
in the wired room & speaking freely \ personnel getting
personal \ the latin word for blister \ a problem
holding a pen with technology \ an advertising campaign
all over town \ buy buy buy \ a dollar dropped
on the street \ hooker-boots in a constant state
of zipping \ stay awhile & leave your shoes
by the bed \ a map redrawn in your head \ a part
of town you frequent \ lines sketched or skipped
depending on urgency \ the persistent unlatching
of a door \ a plunger a work of art \ last chance
to get in on the ground level
in the hurry of morning \ what to do with loose change
in a jacket pocket \ a jagged black line & what looks
like water \ a towering excuse for windows \ all night
owls \ as if we need more sound \ pink neon signs
bleeding on a street \ the paranoid are out
& roaming \ off-course & coarse words bluing
a woman \ to take things beyond running \ a vice
not advice \ to make the blood vessels in your face
upset \ a murder of crows is enough
in the stomach & living it up \ suddenly in the opposite
direction of friction & falling \ abominable not
bomb-able \ sanskrit for a mirror & a wrong
righted \ cain & able not cane-able \ to build a house

of sand on stilts \ a missing spot on a painting
of a leopard \ ascent to the middle not assent to
goodbye \ forever is a word \ odds & ends to amplify
a room \ a window in the woods with glass everywhere
& an orange plastic vibrator \ move move move \ a point
without making \ Eve ate not evacuate \ a good oral
surgeon a necessity \ adieu not i do
in the belly of the wreck a vast scattering of books \ here
come the machines & they taste like salt \ a manner
almost human \ fungi not fun guy \ a haze used to
the ticking \ to trick a believer \ a way to win not
a weigh in \ bet bet bet \ more than one way
to lose it \ a blanket of bugs \ a marked man in
a season of flesh \ apologies all around & a toast
to the fly on the wall \ a bucket of division & no
reason to multiply \ sensible shoes & a reason to
drive drive drive \ a loud silence in the bedroom
not allowed to escape \ the way i remember it

FADE TO PLAN

Shall I move to a sewer (sue
her?)? She might like it. I like
the anonymity of living alone

together (we leave our
fingerprints everywhere).
A house is not enough

to live in. A bird in the hand
is better than a snake.
Say something odd like

the way to a woman's heart
is through her ribcage
(they're taping all of this

so watch what you say).
How's that for romance?
What if I move to a spot

in urbania? May I
manage to age in a place
where there may not be

a plan? Give me a map
to a place where kids
aren't killers (we leave

our fingerprints everywhere).
Now the bombs have faces
(phases?). Crackdown. Crack-

up. Laugh away. Suburbia
may be out of date (dating
is out of date?). There are

plenty of fish in the sea.
There's a new one born
every minute. I prefer

sweaters. Screamers wake
the neighbors. Clothing
is optional (they're taping

all of this, so watch
what you say). Always begin
an advance into the rare

end. If a woman is water
a man is mud. Escape.
Clean up. Find religion. Isn't it

universal? Investigate.
(We leave our fingerprints
everywhere.) Look—

if you're going to burn
the flag, burn the Bible.
Hell, it's on the banned

books list. We have our civic
duty and we are young.
Treason. Heresy. (Watch

what you say. They're taping
all of this.) Deny. Deny.
Deny. Construct a plan

and gather the innocent.
Seep into every street
in every city. Only details

are remembered. I need
an agony bone. She needs
a voice bone. How

romantic. All that matters
is the action inherent
in the bedroom. Here it

comes. You bet. Sex is
complex. Vowels stick
together (we leave

our fingerprints
everywhere). We are
the ultimate expression

(impression?) of what
it means to be dying
minute by minute, dripping

out of silence, waking
and stranded in a sewer
of our own making.

5 CRACKS

I'm not saying she deserved it, but by
no means was she innocent. Who the fuck
is innocent? Are you innocent?
You have a Ph.D. in pissing
people off. Back then I didn't know
what the fuck I was doing. I was like
some amateur trainee salesman or
something. But I learned the game.
I played it. You get to know it
quick. Out there you either learn fast
or you're dead by daybreak.

*   *   *   *

It's always on a rookie's block that a fight breaks out. They test him, you know? One guy jumps somebody, and the rest watch to see how the rookie handles it. Best thing to do is just beat the holy hell out of both of them. That sends a message. They see you don't mess around with fights, that you can handle yourself, and you get a reputation right then. Next time they think twice. My man Teddy, when he was a rookie—first day on the job—one guy shanks this Irishman in the yard. Opened up his belly in one swipe. Died right there. Teddy, he pounces on this guy, grabs the knife before the rest of us even know what's going on. I think he jerked the guy's shoulder out of its socket. Personally, I believe we're here to keep the peace, sort of like weed killers keeping the garden green, you know?

*   *   *   *

The first time it was easy.
I didn't even pull the trigger.
He was scared. Gave it up.
He was crying like a little bitch.
Money runs quick on the outside
but the living is slow.
You got to make something
happen. I remember one time
I was in and out of a house
in one minute flat. I timed it.

Those were the easy days. Money
was easy. The slugs didn't know me
then. I was small time, but I got big
quick. One day I was fucked-up,
hustling for a hamburger,
and the next I had the whole street
in my pocket. I was hooked.
I had track marks from all
the money in me.

*　　　*　　　*　　　*

When he was seven, Ronnie threw Joseph
down the stairs, dislocating his shoulder.
It's the sort of thing that happens
between brothers. Ronnie never knew his own
strength. One time, while I was cleaning
his room, I looked out the window and saw him
tear away the metal fencing from a steel pole
running into the Warren's backyard.
It was something about that dog of theirs.
He always liked that dog—liked to tease him
anyway. If Ronnie was nearby, that Husky
would know it. His ears would pop up, his eyes
shifting like he knew something was about
to happen—like how they say animals always know
when it's about to storm. With that dog
on his leash, Ronnie ran up, kicked him
in his side, and slipped away before those teeth
grabbed him. I watched him a couple minutes—
figured he'd get his fill of it—but finally
I had to yell for him to leave that dog alone.
Sometimes little boys don't know their limits.
He came back to our yard with the Husky's bone
in his hand. I made him give it back.

*　　　*　　　*　　　*

I don't mind talking about it.
It's already been done. Already
been said. They made sure of that.

You ever wonder what it's like
          to burn a man's eyes out?
                    It's a thing to see.
          After a while in the game
     you get a gut feeling
when the guy looking you dead
     in the eyes isn't playing
          by the same rules. A man
                    has to be punished for breaking
          rules. Everybody, everything—
     from fish to fortune tellers—
has rules. The whole fucking
     universe has them. It's all
          circular. It all comes back to you.

          *   *   *   *

                    I knew Ron before all this mess.
                    He's the type of man who's as good
                    as he is bad—the type you always
                    hear about on TV. He'd treat me

                    like I was all that mattered in this
                    whole sorry state—like a princess
                    or something. Then ten minutes later
                    he'd be turning over furniture, nailing

                    the end of a gun to my forehead.
                    Even after that—and the terrible things
                    he did to that woman—I can't say
                    I don't still feel something for him.

                    One morning he was gone, gone like rain
                    down a gutter. He took my stereo, my car,
                    some money. I thought I was in love.
                    A note said he'd be back in a couple weeks.

          *   *   *   *

Take this Mitchell
for instance. He burned me
on a whole heap of money—
so I burned his eyes out
with a cigarette lighter.
It's that easy. It's all
circular. Everything comes
back around. I'm a living fucking
example. They put me here
for what I did out in the world
they made. I belong here.
I broke their rules,
so now they're burning out
my eyes every day—every
day I'm staring at these
bars. Hell, I did so much
evil shit—the state of Texas
couldn't do enough to get even.
They try though. Just as much
fucked-up shit happens in here
as on the outside. You just don't
hear about it. Last month,
middle of the night, a guy
gets set on fire in his cell.
Nobody saw nothing. He didn't
even scream. Now *that's* balls.

*   *   *   *

In here, the first thing you have to remember is that *you're* in charge. If they start to think you're afraid, or even unwilling to crack their heads, if necessary, they're going to take advantage—and that's trouble for everybody. They can smell a rookie like chow time, like dogs. I don't know what it is. I remember when I first got here. I was scared to death. At first they give you looks, you know, like they're sizing you up. You have to stare them down, look through them—through the walls into the outside. Once they think you're weak, it's all over.

*   *   *   *

                            If you ask me, that bitch
deserved it as much as any
                    punk junky. She'd been
                                asking for it, and she got
                                        what she got. One night
                            she was helping me sell
                some rock. Come to find out
most of it was going up
                her nose. I still don't
                        know how much money
                                    she stole from me. Too
                        much. Shit. I didn't mean
                to do her though.
It just got emotional,
                you know? She had to pay
                        with something. She was
                                as good and bad as anybody.
                    I did her like they're doing me
            now. That night she probably
didn't even know what planet
            she was on. She was too
                    fucked-up to give it up.
                                So I took it. Then she
                    thought she was just gonna
            leave. Shit just got out of hand.

                *   *   *   *

It's true that Ronnie stole a neighbor's car
when he was just fifteen. It was after Joseph's
operation on his eye. But Ronnie didn't make it
across the border into Mexico. The police
picked him up in Crystal City. He was strange
in those days. Drugs or something. It got to the point
where John and I were at wits end. We didn't know
what to do. Looking back, he should have been
locked up right then. It's hard to lose hope
on your own, though—and we didn't.
His sophomore year of high school they put him
on the honor roll. That's something. But after that
it was mostly 2 a.m. bailouts and beatings
from John. At that age you can't very well

- 44 -

hit a kid anymore. He'd had plenty, and one night
he let John know it. Ronnie was as big
or bigger by then, and they got into some kind
of tussle. Before I got to the basement, Ronnie
had him on the ground and against the wall, shouting
I'm gonna kill him. He looked up and our eyes
met. Then he just let go of John and walked
out of the house. That was nearly 20 years ago.

         *   *   *   *

Now they're gonna give me what
I got coming. We're trading lives
for lives, like money. That's what
I am. Money. What are you?
It's people like you—buying us
all up—saving day after day like
there's some big fucking payoff,
some big collection plate at the end
of your imaginary rainbow.
I'm here to tell you we're full
and spilling over. Listen. I'm telling
you I'm ready—ready
for all the pain you got.
You can strap us in chairs,
turn us on—but what happens
when there ain't enough
juice to go around? Are you
gonna chop off our heads
and drag us around the city
like they used to do? I want
my head cut off and stuck on the
Don't Mess With Texas sign.

         *   *   *   *

Sometimes this place feels like the streets. Even though I'm the one with the
stick, usually it's me who's watching over his shoulder. I leave these walls
every night and go home to my wife, just like anybody else—a banker or a
school teacher—but somehow I never leave this place. It crawls under my
skin, wraps me up like this uniform.

*   *   *   *

I don't think he should get it. I know he's done
some bad, terrible things. But Ronnie still has *some*
good in him. He wasn't always bad. He's got to pay
for what he's done, but that doesn't mean
he should be killed. He knows he did wrong.
He knows Jesus, and he knows the way of the sheep
in slaughter. I don't know what we did wrong.
I don't know what we didn't do. All I know
is Ronnie couldn't have done all those things.
He was raised better than that. After he left
he got in with some bad people, but he never
could have done *that*. I'm not saying he's innocent.
He's guilty. They showed it. But I can't believe
he cut up that girl like that, took her unborn
baby girl away, her life. He couldn't.
He told me he didn't—looked me in my eyes.

*   *   *   *

It's going on out there right now.
                You bet. Down the alleys,
          up the stairways, in bedrooms,
     even out in the wide, wild
open. Right this second
          a man's throat is being
               slashed, another's thick
                    head torn open by a bullet.
          Nobody's gonna stop it. They're
     gonna have to put
a fence around Texas and lock
     everybody up. People lose
          their heads out here
                in the desert. People get
          desert brains. Only the outlaws survive.

*   *   *   *

september   *the fall*   *outside*

     alive   *front door*   *swung*

     open   *twisted*   *hinges*

frozen wind   *against*

     this stomach   *hot*

     flowing   *out*

sticky   *swollen carpet*   *cold cut*

     phone cord   *my mother*

     in nevada   *my daughter my*

mother   *my stomach*   *one more*

     one   *rough*

red ceiling   *wait*   *wait*

     hard rain   *rains*

     red bricks   *brown*   *wait*

     voices   *in the walls*

     are cracking

PERPETUAL NOTION

WET PAINT

Now the windows are blue and the doors have stopped
shouting. The glass has been carved to its bones

and there is a garden inside. The carving happens
as many things happen, and sometimes we just have to

face it when the house loses its stories and its beds
become rivers. Out in the yard, grass bends

into the slender face of a girl. Grass can be difficult
and daughters don't return. The garden rolls

over and it's winter and the house has a river running
through it. A face being stored in an attic is dusted

and tried on. A color-spotted smock, once used
for painting, is unpacked and hung about the body.

Its frayed white rope is tied as many things are tied.
Outside the snow falls easily and no one seems to notice.

In front of a fire an easel has been set and many brushes
lined up. A son phones from the East Coast. Old paint

colors the shallow dark of a shoebox. Polaroids fade.
The man on the radio has given up. Outside the grass

won't be taken, and it's comforting considering how
quick the cold moves. In a season sometime soon, the garden

will wake and the river will change as many things change—
and even paint might lose its body and finally find its way.

MY WEIGHT IN CHANGE

Without our knowing, our voices
leave us and disappear
into the hypnotic, humming

crowd. We lay our money
down on our futures and expect
grace from our pasts. Fathers

remind us of our inadequacies
while speaking of road sign metaphors
and techniques necessary

for succession. The more insightful quote
Ginsberg at family gatherings
while the bitter and unfulfilled

shout at television politicians. Mothers
stand dutifully with hands on hips
and communicate discomfort

intensely with gestures of the face.
The more provoked demand divorce
while the bitter and unfulfilled

take matters into their own hands.
Some of the more aspiring ones
make television news with stories

of cock carvings. Children hover
like determined moths, holding close
to fighting words like nuggets

of gold, selling them to playgrounds
in furious sentences
while marauding through suburbia

blankly, learning of the power
of confusion. When nights get too tiresome
we find ourselves in beds on top

of one another. We maneuver
into the darkness of opposite edges.
Morning forces us into cumbersome

identities. We step over our usual
ten-dollar worn-out excuses, trip over
the unknowable, and pretend

we understand the reasons
for our disillusionment. We are concerned
about our insolent beginnings,

though not enough to give in
to the constant bidding, absolute need
for the win, some discovery. We set

alarms, brush teeth, wait
for buses, eat cheeseburgers
and drink beer. We're all waiting for

what's next. A mother's death. Your best
friend's job promotion or your sworn
enemy's. Coffee, a shot of whiskey,

or both. If there is such a thing
as a real home, we may be shocked
to open doors to the weather

within. We should expect our instincts
to be flawed. We should expect to be
disappointed, to disappoint countless

others. We should count on missing
the mark and swallowing the point
once in a while. We imagined being

settled on the moon by now, or at least
to have vacationed there. We watched
Armstrong and the others. We're tired

of television news. We want
promises kept and expectations fulfilled.
We want to be part of something

big. We've waited our whole lives.
We want to build fires
and write books. We want to sit

on the edges of seats. We're ready
to swallow down anything
to take the edge off, to take us

anywhere else. We're ready to believe
in anything. We wonder what
ever happened to time-travel, or at least

the possibility of it. If we have to spend
one quarter more to see
a movie, we're going to riot

in the streets. We're small, but growing.
Sometimes we just want to drive
all night, drink a gallon of beer, and think

we're getting away with something.
I'm sick of wondering what the rest of you
are doing. I'm tired of shifting

this anxiousness through dark, empty rooms.
My eyes are half-open, glass
cracked, but holding on. Where are we

going next? It's not too late.
It's time to get a bunch of us
into space. We like to see things

for ourselves. There must be
something we haven't discovered yet.
Let's lose our minds and spend

the rest of our lives looking. I'm tired
and I haven't eaten since I learned
of my insignificance. I've been waiting

for more senses, tense and counting
clouds. I've asked questions
with no answers. What is

the nineteenth wonder of the world?
I've spent countless, indescribable lives
alone, long moments wrapped up

in women, nights digging through piles
of paper, hours curled up
on mattresses. I've spent

too long thinking about desire, wandering
curiously on, still wondering if ever
I'll figure my weight in change.

ON SONNETS

1.

Halloween

After all of the wrappers are empty, they stop
in the park behind the elementary school.
The sky opens and rain throws its body into
the slippery distance between them. They slide head-
first down the wet, grassy hill. Her cherry chapstick
and red spiral licorice melt into the light
of the harvest moon. The fresh, red superman stamp
on the back of his hand and his frayed bedroom cape
cling like new skin. They blink in the heavy autumn
air and touch their greasy mouths together. Lips
quiver warm and sticky. Her muddy hands muddy
his. Rain hangs from the ends of their eyelashes.
Her hair is yellow and soft, like a girl should be.
His sugary finger makes her tremble and shine.

2.

Letter to a Boy

If you have a beard, spray-paint the word *tough* on it.
If you don't have a beard, grow one. Read the story
of Ahab. Whatever you do, don't join the army.
But learn to fire a weapon. You never know what
you might someday stand for. Write revealing letters.
Never sign your name. Let your fingernails grow wild
like weeds. Eat big bowls of raw meat. It will make you
strong. Do not let your mouth get you punched in the gut.
Tell your father you forgive him for the time he
got drunk and hit-on your girlfriend. Get a woman
to write her name on your arm. If the ink washes
off in the morning, she didn't press hard enough.
Know how far you'll go. Then go further. Above all,
keep a secret that is unimaginable.

3.

Housing

Grown pains, a push, stretched out. Bodies
helped up, knocked down. Less rain but more
rust. Women decide whose hand goes
down whose pants, what to keep and when.
Men about to lose it. How hard
it is, how easy. A western sky

sweats, deposits. Still, aren't we all
becoming young? In our sticky
collisions are there spaces for
the little light we shed? We belong
somewhere? Perpetual notion
of pursuit, the body's last request,
these houses we must leave to live in.
There is still time to become us.

THREAD

On the way to see the pagans
we stopped to buy a dictionary.

The street was one long curb
and the buildings evicted.

It would be easy to tell you
the street signs were wrong.

If the west wasn't won
it would have moved here.

Words were metal in our mouths
and our fingertips rubbed off.

It would be wrong
to give you the impression.

If the clocks were right
the past didn't go anywhere.

The tumbleweed was only a weed
before our arrival.

It would be hard to tell
whether the faces were real.

If our hands were handles
we'd already be open.

You would know what it was
to be carnivorous and mean it.

It would be right around the corner
and up the block on your left.

If you had an egg for every orgasm
you'd be scrambled.

On the way to buy a dictionary
the pagans stopped to see us.

DRAWING THE LINE

1.

Mississippi John Hurt hits the chorus of "It Ain't
Nobody's Business," and it occurs to me I may relive you
in another life, another impression. Tilt of bone, grudge
of skin, another moment like this moment—always that
but not this moment. Today is rain tapping the roof
like a shoulder, a reminder of all worth remembering—
every joke's punch-line, every moral of the story.
To relive is to de-cycle. Recycle and de-live.
We're doing our best at this stage, acting the part, singing
the song like we know it. When the smoke clears
I'll be small and bony, wear a beard to my navel—
my body-salt a thing to be measured and exchanged for
on some misguided side of the black market.

2.

You live off the land, a diet of leaves and fruit ripening
in the steely light of your hands—your body a thing
to be studied, painted, and recreated in sculpture—a thing
even I may shy away from. The small moments of your body
sculpted and hardened, sent out on display from country
to country, a work of art in an artwork world.
The past barely passed, as if what we do, what we
become in each strained, diabolical romance is the work
of infidels and whores. Still, the unbelievable transforms
the real, even as the ink of the critic's quick pen dries
down another lie we laugh at—our little lives, how we
create and perform the black spit of our lungs and guts.
A hammer pop-pops our teeth out, two-by-two—that lump
blossoming in the throat and giving in to what hurts us.

3.

The way we live down the sky, heavy soil still smoldering—
a reason to plan and plant. The environmentalists
calling themselves environmentalists on every channel,
the rest of us falling a few feet shy of the recycling bin.
What's left are the swashbuckling steel-shouldered
nuclear guts of the big-rigs grinding up sky and inching
their way to the flushing grounds of Yucca Mountain.
We scramble to the forests, shovels in hand. Someone opens
a can of green paint. The wooly men of the pack pull
their shirts off, the gathering women rushing up behind them
to paint the word "NATURAL" down the spines of their backs.
We dig and dig, shouting a chorus at the trucks grumbling
towards us: "URANIUM IN YER CRANIUM! URANIUM
IN YER CRANIUM! URANIUM IN YER CRANIUM!"

4.

Up ahead they've dug a hole. As if death was a real
moment, we toss ourselves in and start up with "It Ain't
Nobody's Business." Above us they hit that note, that one
note that survives us. Finally dawn breaks—as if anyone
deserves it—and we climb out into what we are. We hold
the seeds of death in our hands, the dying part of us
that lives on, the light that outlives us. We go on
like usual: Head in the Clouds versus Head in the Dirt.
Work continues as planned. We push our way into lines.
Over there a line of filing cabinets. Beyond them a line
of shredders. The sound of a hush cuts a whisper in half.
Then the circling sounds of pens on paper—the way we
rewrite our names the same way, each day, always.

KUDZU

When kudzu
finally grabs
ground
on the other side
of the house, we work
the knife, digging
our way
clear of the living room.
Indiana woods
whisper the way
lovers do—
hallowed art
of seduction.
Barely spared, I reach
through thick
soil, fingernails
caked and clawed
bloody, the glare
of grandfather trees
crusted in light.
Mother pulls
dirt from her hair.
Father breaks
branches.
No one speaks.
A fire is built.
We take turns
staring at one another.
No one sleeps.
Night slips away
into morning.
Our bodies become
wet
and ensnared
in the webbed
dripping of roots.
Oh—
the groan of its guts,
its roving hooves
of hunger, our daily
ration of rage.

TRANSMISSION

In Memory of David Chandler

Four Corvette tires stuck to a gray floor
and November isn't going anywhere soon.
That woman, the alcohol, the buckets of pills
sent you stumbling into the garage, into that hole
of a car, that everyman's dream. You listened
to the motor fire up on one turn and hum steadily,
grumbling for a road. But then you pulled down
that heavy door easily, and it must have startled you
at first. An impossible crack of light lined the edge
of the garage. Then the air got so thick
you could feel the weight of the car in your ears.
With one hand on the wheel you scribbled
war words to her on a scrap of paper. I wonder
how long your body waited there, if it ever
occurred to you to jerk that transmission into
reverse and bust back through that dark door.
Eventually the gas burned out and she was drunk
when she found you. The Corvette was already primed
and in the corner were the cans of cherry paint
you would have hung on her. Finally some man
muscled up that door. Your breaths lingering there
disappeared wildly into the sun. They said
you never would have done that, but how
could they know how completely you could
lose yourself in the greasy logic of machinery?

A SHORT HISTORY OF US

1. The Beginning

When we were nothing, we were only
color. *White* unrolled

a canvas. *Red* seized language and wrote.
Orange collided with

sound. *Yellow* went straight for the nose.
Blue captured bodies

and spread *Green* on them. *Purple* came
for desire, and it clung

close to the body. *Gray* wanted evidence.
Black found a heart.

2. The Past

I called you *woman*, and you said *man—*
and that was good

enough. We'd no idea we were building
a past. You, then

I, opened the dark with eyes narrowed
in criminal frustration.

And afterwards, wrapped up like dead
dogs, we really loved

each other—until our sweat completely
melted into the sheets.

3. The Present

This moment is now that moment.
You tried to grab

and squeeze it, but it was the sound
of a motorcycle

passing. The next is the last—your
past transformed

like cells. Now look at what you've
done. Wait for

the heave of your chest—the push
out—then in.

4. The Future

When the heat finally hits Fahrenheit
451, the gray

smoke will lick and sting our faces
black. Books

will pile fifty stories high into jagged
pyramids. Words

will attach to the rising body of smoke.
Sentences will

drift into paragraphs painted sharply
on a burnt sky.

5. The Great Beyond

Light and color are memories. Sound
is the only sensation.

Crossing over is like finding your way
through the dark

of a room you've always known.
Silence is furious

before wind. Hear it breathe reasons
for waiting until

now. Afterwards, music is heavy and
unstoppable. Listen.

After the Theatre

You're an asshole, she said.
I'm sick of it.

He wanted to disagree
but her hips were right

there, ripe and bursting
from the folds of her

red dress, and the way
she held her mouth like that

made him think of his mother.
He was creeped-

out and loving it and
I know, he said.

Sometimes just saying it
makes it real.

He scrunched his left eye
closed, slid right hand

over right: navigating
the slit. He asked her to do it

and she did
and they stood there

in the living room
almost looking at each other.

THE ARMPIT OF DESIRE

1.

Finally the racers
spin into the track's
concrete wall, making
atomic contact, scraps
of fiberglass rocketing
across the field—
the best pinball game
ever, the rush of adrenaline
indescribable, whatever
the vantage point.
From a distance there's no
human element. Pure desire
for carnage. Just that.
Extent of injuries and death
an unspoken high-five,
what it's all about.

2.

Silence is written on the walls. Linoleum
doesn't burn well. Drywall is punctured
where a head should be. Smoke has chalked
its battered outline on the ceiling. Everywhere
the stench of construction. The man
tracing clouds on the roof is howling
the word Lisa and steadying the chimney.
Surely somewhere there's about to be
a solar eclipse, or at least a star
numbered and named after some woman
quietly shooting its blurry way into oblivion.

3.

Sometimes it all starts with a morning prayer.
Knees and elbows and mouths begin anything.
The part of you that believes, the soft
belly of desire—take it into your hands.

In the distance between the part of you that feels
and the part of you that knows,
your dreams are alive in the armpit of desire.
They survive you there. There's no way
around it, and finally it's all there is.

4.

On the shoreline
of desire, a book—
its pages turning over
and over in the wind,
but not a single word
written in it.
Off in the distance
a single howl.
Suddenly a splash.
Breath held deep,
down to the feet.
The bluing of a face.

5.

The street blurs into oil. Disintegration
is imaginary. It's August. The cemetery
is a place to go. On one of the taller stones
a man stands on his head, his body
shivering. Sweat has woven itself
into the cotton of his shirt. A girl-child appears
and runs as if for the first time. She finally
wears out in the tall, rubbery grass
and pushes him over with one hand.
Their breath can't be caught. Bugs bite
and then chew. It would be a good time
to pray for rain. The sky shrinks a little
on a summer day when you think
you've been forgotten. Then a girl-child
sees your stone and thinks it's pretty.

6.

It's habit, now. You choke down
your daily lozenge of desire.
It's red hot no matter where you live.
You're out the door and on the street,
that wily smile widening your face
and tonguing that one word—covet—
and then again—covet—in your mouth.
Each crack in the sidewalk stepped over
is an accomplishment—every movement
a type of tool and memory a form of grace.
Every woman is a scalding of the throat
and every man a knot in the stomach.
Those were the days, you think, when your body
took whatever you gave it, when each night
you were out before your head hit the pillow.
Love the past as if it can remember.

978-0-595-36882-2
0-595-36882-4

Printed in the United States
36849LVS00007B/562-663

9 780595 368822